HAND PAINTED ROYAL WORCESTER PORCELAIN

The Golden Years

AUTHORS

PETER MARSH AND CRAIG SMITH

THE ROYAL PORCELAIN WORKS

Published by Peter Marsh and Craig Smith.
P.O. Box 3898 Sheffield S36 0AH.

ISBN 0-9551012-0-4

This book is available directly from

Peter Marsh	Craig Smith
P.O. Box 3898	P.O. Box 165
Sheffield S36 0AH	74 Railway Avenue
South Yorkshire	East Ringwood 3135
United Kingdom	Victoria Australia
Email peterpmarsh@aol.com	Email royalwor@bigpond.net.au

Please contact us to include pieces in future editions of this book.

Acknowledgements
We would like to extend our grateful thanks to the following, without whose support this book would not have been possible:

Annabel Watts, David and Valerie Main, Graham at Abcir, Peter Woodger, Sally Marsh, Narelle Smith, Jane Cartledge, Ian Taylor, Richard Bridges, Elio Rulli and Chantelle Iacuone.

Designed and Typeset by Whoosh Design Graphics Limited
www.whooshdesign.co.uk

Printed in Great Britain by
Caric Press Ltd. Bournemouth
www.caricpress.co.uk

Contents

Introductions 4

Foreword 6

A Brief History 7

Harry Davis 8

Charles Baldwyn 32

John Stinton 50

Fruit Painters 70

George Owen 84

William Hawkins 96

Richard Sebright 106

Walter Powell 114

Harry Stinton 122

Frank Roberts 128

James Stinton 134

William Powell 140

Edward Salter 144

Loving Cup 146

Walter Sedgley 148

Kitty Blake 150

Raymond Rushton 152

George Johnson 154

Frederick Chivers 156

John Ayrton 158

Coronation Orbs 159

George Cole 160

Ernest Phillips 161

Harry Chair 162

Josiah Rushton 163

Ernest Barker 164

George Evans 165

James Bradley 166

Robert Perling 167

William Jarman 168

Harry Martin 169

Jack Southall 170

Charles White 171

Advertisements 172

Date Codes 175

Index 176

Introduction

FOR MANY YEARS, Royal Worcester porcelain has been seriously collected to the point of it becoming an obsession. 'Worcesteritis' the wife calls it, and believe me she's right. We all strive for the best and rarest pieces; we battle it out in auction rooms around the world, getting up at all hours for telephone bids, all for the right pieces for our collection - but boy it is worth it.

The Royal Worcester factory in the early 1900s to 1941, did something that will never be repeated. They collected all the finest ceramic artists in the country and sat them in paint rooms painting their wares - from fruit, sheep, Highland cattle, game birds, cows, swans, polar bears, castles, gardens - the list goes on and on. This group of painters could turn their hand to any subject and carry it out to an amazing standard. They lived for their paintings and studied their subjects on their days off, some exhibiting at the Royal Academy.

Royal Worcester porcelain, to me, is the finest in the world - each piece signed and dated giving it a unique identity; each piece painted as a one off - a collector's dream. The Stinton Highland cattle on the misty Scottish heather strewn moors can never be repeated; the Baldwyn flying swans skimming the river Severn in Worcester can never be done the same way again; the remoteness of the Harry Davis sheep high up in the hills with their lambs - all lost to time but living on in the form of vases, plates and plaques, exchanging hands for thousands of pounds but always holding their value when given up.

The pieces that live on today are the very pieces that I want to bring to everybody's collection in the form of this book.

This book is dedicated to my dear friend Glynn Morris who died of cancer on the 4th March 2005, aged 39.

PETER MARSH

Introduction

ROYAL WORCESTER PORCELAIN inspires a passion that is surprising and difficult to comprehend at times. However, when a collection is compiled together in a book such as this, you realize that the reverence is warranted. Individually, the pieces feature magnificent painting, intricate gilding, majestic shapes and vibrant colours - all with great attention to detail. Combining with a wonderful synergy, a piece of Royal Worcester can approach porcelain perfection - the final result being a thing of beauty that will stand the test of time. Add in the work of George Owen and the Royal Worcester Golden Years become evident.

After many years of repeatedly searching through old auction house catalogues, looking for shapes and particular examples of Royal Worcester, we decided a book such as this would be useful. Given the paucity of books with good colour photographs of a subject as visually striking as Royal Worcester, it seemed a good opportunity to compile a collection of fine pieces. We have tried to be representative of the artists, styles and shapes, as well as including some rare and unusual examples. It is not exhaustive and the confines of space and cost mean that many worthwhile examples are not included.

We hope to do future editions along similar lines and we realize there are many pieces around the world that warrant a place in a book such as this. To this end, we would welcome any contact from fellow Royal Worcester collectors who feel they have some worthy examples. This can be done anonymously and confidentiality is assured. Please see page 2 for our contact details.

We hope this book is useful as a comprehensive reference manual as well as bringing you many years of enjoyment and pleasure.

CRAIG SMITH

Foreword

My wife and I have dealt in quality Royal Worcester porcelain for almost 20 years, specializing particularly in the hand painted and artist signed field. During this time, we have often discussed the need for a good book illustrating a wide variety of shapes and specialty subjects by the many talented artists.

This illustrative work is a tribute to the dedication of the authors, Peter Marsh and Craig Smith, in researching the many shapes and styles available, obtaining images, illustrating and producing what promises to be valued reference book for Royal Worcester collectors worldwide.

It's been a long time coming, but we feel this book achieves everything we have discussed over the years and highlights what we believe to be Royal Worcester's finest years - the early to mid 20th century.

DAVID AND VALERIE MAIN

Worcester Royal Porcelain Company – A Brief History

IN JUNE 1751, the Worcester Porcelain Company was established by Dr. John Wall and William Davis with fifteen other partners. They began to manufacture porcelain at the Warmstry House factory on the banks of the River Severn.

The years 1751-1776 were known as the 'Dr. Wall' period and encompassed the time at the factory until the death of Dr. Wall in 1776.

Davis then continued to run the factory until his death in 1783, after which Thomas Flight bought the factory - the years 1776-1793 were known as the 'Davis/Flight' years.

In 1793, Flight was joined at the factory by Martin Barr, meaning that the years 1793-1807 became known as the 'Flight and Barr' period.

A family change in 1807, resulted in the period 1807-1813 being known as the 'Barr, Flight and Barr' period.

The years 1813-1840 were then known as the 'Flight, Barr and Barr' period.

In 1840, 'Flight, Barr and Barr' amalgamated with 'Chamberlain' (another Worcester porcelain factory in operation since 1786) and became 'Chamberlain and Co.' All production was then moved to the Chamberlain's factory at Diglis.

In 1852, W. H. Kerr and R. W. Binns purchased 'Chamberlain and Co.' and changed the name of the company to 'Kerr & Binns'.

In 1862, Kerr retired and Binns formed a joint stock company called 'Worcester Royal Porcelain Company Limited' which is what is commonly known as Royal Worcester and is still in existence today.

In 1889, Royal Worcester purchased another Worcester porcelain factory called 'Grainger and Co.' which they had completely amalgamated with by 1902.

In 1896, Royal Worcester bought a second porcelain factory in Worcester called 'James Hadley and Sons' and had completely amalgamated with it by 1905.

Royal Worcester is still in production at the current time in 2005.

Harry Davis

ALTHOUGH HE WOULD get a lot of competition from Charles Baldwyn and John Stinton, Harry Davis was probably the 'name' painter to have worked at Royal Worcester - and he worked there for an astonishing 71 years. His versatility and talent will never be seen again and his work is always in great demand. The quality of his painting is exceptional, whether on porcelain or as a watercolour.

Born in 1885, Harry started at the factory on his thirteenth birthday. He came from a family long known to the factory. His father Alfred worked in the pressing room and his grandfather Josiah was a gilder with a fine reputation.

After spending the first year doing menial tasks around the factory, Harry was apprenticed to the talented Edward Salter, striking up a strong friendship with him. Both were keen fisherman and they often sketched the fish they caught.

Harry had been taught drawing by his grandfather and had a natural talent. He excelled as a painter of sheep, fish, birds, cottages, castles, scenes of London and figural objects. Landscape painting had always attracted him, particularly in the classical style of Claude and the melting colourings of Corot. He was noted for his brilliant portrayals of sheep in Scottish Highland scenes, even though he had never actually been there (a holiday given to him by the factory as a reward for 70 years of service had to be cancelled due to his wife's death). It seems that Harry could paint any subject he wanted - extending his repertoire to depicting animals as unusual as horses, deer, pigs and even polar bears!

After the retirement of William Hawkins in 1928, Harry was appointed as foreman painter and as such was responsible for the introduction of many etchings that were made to teach the trainees how to paint and colour in.

The colouring in of pre-painted outlines was a routine practice at Worcester and most other porcelain factories. Harry was responsible for his own share of this, but he was very conscious of the difference to free hand painting, signing this type of work 'H. Sivad', which is, of course, a reversal of his name.

Harry has great many works to his credit - amongst them, the double service for the Maharaja Ranjitsinji and the colour standard for Doris Lindner's figure of Princess Elizabeth on Tommy, which he did from life at Buckingham Palace.

He was a man of unfailing courtesy, amazed that anyone would be interested in him or his work - an honest and conscientious craftsman of great integrity.

At the age of 69, Harry retired as foreman in 1954. However, he continued to work at the factory until a few months before his death in 1970, aged 84.

A magnificent bough pot painted with sheep in the Scottish Highlands,
signed H. Davis, dated 1911, shape 1428, standing 35cm high.

The pair to the vase pictured on the opposite page.

An exceptional cobalt blue vase painted in the style of Claude,
signed H. Davis, dated 1919, shape number 2406, 33cm high.

A important vase painted with a stag and deer in the Scottish Highlands,
signed H. Davis, dated 1907, shape 1969, 51cm high.

An excellent rose jar painted with sheep in a meadow,
signed H. Davis, dated 1928, shape 2048, 25cm high.

A rare painting of shire horses by Harry Davis, dated 1906,
in the ever popular 1969 shape, 40cm high.

A magnificent vase painted with sheep looking out over a Scottish loch,
signed H. Davis, dated 1924, shape H314, 27cm high.

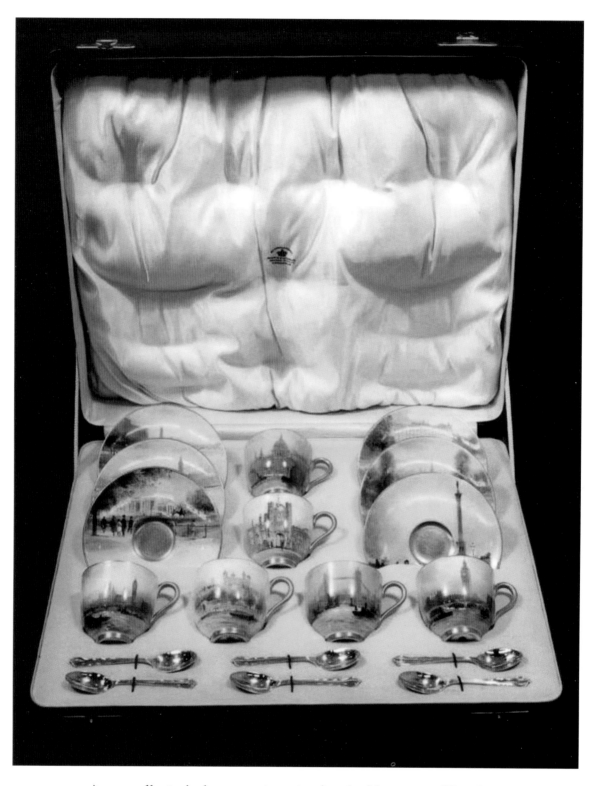

A rare collector's dream - a tea set painted with scenes of London,
signed Harry Davis, dated 1925.

A large exhibition quality cobalt blue vase painted with a country scene,
signed H. Davis, dated 1911, shape 1969, 52cm high.

A good plaque painted with sheep in the Scottish Highlands,
signed H. Davis, dated 1920, 10cm diameter.

A blush shape 1515 painted with sheep,
signed H. Davis, dated 1911, 17cm high.

A very rare pair of plaques by Harry Davis depicting sheep and goats,
dated 1927, size 23 by 15cm.

A fine and rare vase painted with polar bears, signed H. Davis,
dated 1903, shape 2256, 26cm high (courtesy of Brian and Wendy Mitton).

A stunning vase painted with sheep overlooking a loch,
signed H. Davis, dated 1908, shape 1572, standing 27cm high.

An excellent pair of pot-pourris signed
H. Davis, dated 1935, shape H175, 12cm high.

A superb pair of sheep vases signed H. Davis,
dated 1917, shape 1762, standing 21cm high.

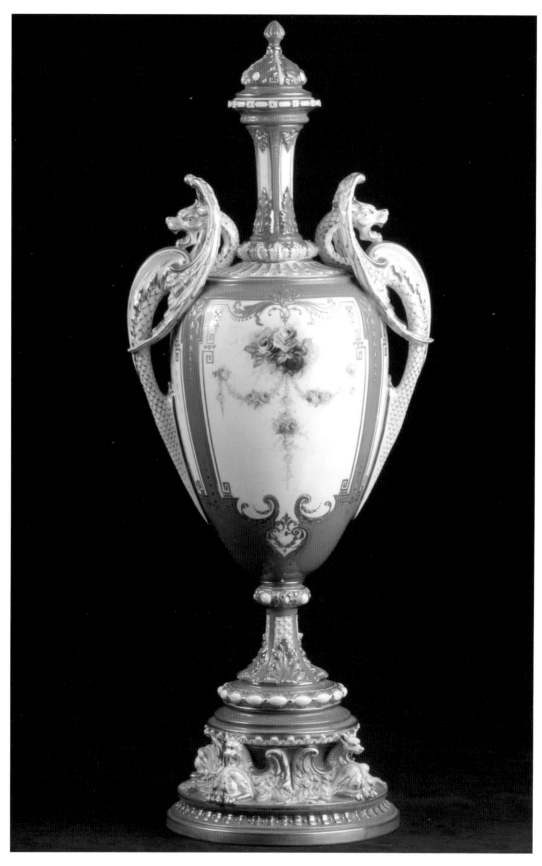

This is the back of the vase pictured on the opposite page,
painted with swags of flowers signed E. Phillips.

A very important exhibition vase painted with a country scene,
signed H. Davis, dated 1905, shape 2090, standing a massive 66cm high.

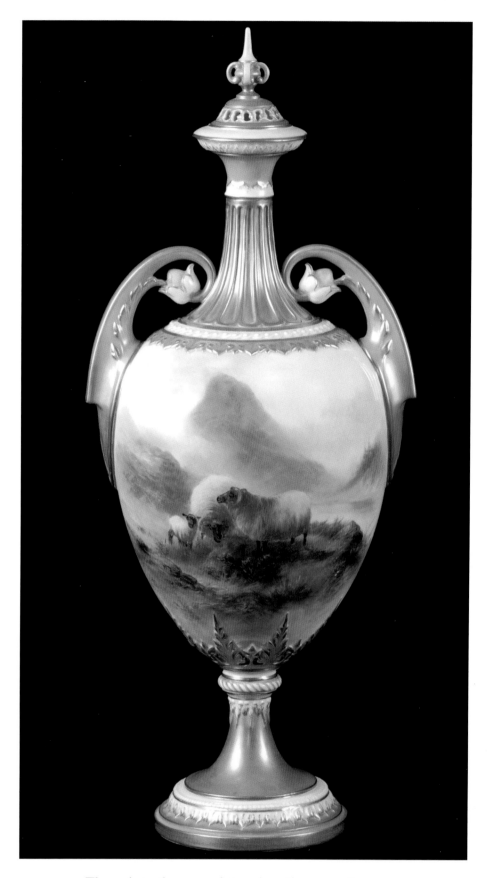

The pair to the vase pictured on the opposite page.

A superb vase painted with sheep in the Scottish Highlands,
signed H. Davis, dated 1910, shape H248, 40cm high.

A very rare painting of pigs in a farm setting by
Harry Davis, dated 1925, shape G957, 9cm high.

A superbly painted vase signed H. Davis, depicting sheep in the
Scottish Highlands, dated 1905, shape G962, standing 23cm high.

A impressive pair of vases painted with scenes from the Lake District England,
on the left is Wray Castle, on the right is Rydal, both signed H. Davis,
dated 1907, shape number 2158, standing 29cm high.

An excellent pot-pourri painted with a scene in the style of Claude,
signed H. Davis, dated 1912, shape 2450, 25cm high.

Charles Baldwyn

THERE CAN BE few ceramic painters better known or respected than Charles Henry Clifford Baldwyn. Or Charley, as he preferred to be called.

His paintings of swans in flight on Royal Worcester vases are his 'signature' pieces and instantly recognisable. His other trademark speciality were paintings of birds in moonlight scenes and during his stay at the factory, no-one else was allowed to paint either of these subjects. His exceptional talent means that Baldwyn's work is now extremely desirable and collectable.

Born in 1859, Baldwyn worked at the Royal Worcester factory from 1874 until 1904. Much of his early work will be unsigned or may bear the monograms 'BY', 'B' or 'CB". Most of these early subjects were birds in moonlight scenes, sometimes with a Japanese influence as was commonplace at the time.

Charley's great love was the local bird life. He would often spend hours out in the countryside with the other painters, sketching small birds in the wild and would buy or borrow captured birds to study. He would then reproduce the scenes on porcelain with great skill.

As with many other painters during these often hard times, Charles would supplement his income by selling watercolours and he also often bought blanks from the factory to paint at home (often in the company of other artists from the factory - a practice presumably frowned upon by the management) and sell them on privately. These would inevitably be signed but not carry the Royal Worcester mark. Apparently, he also painted pieces for other artists to sell and his father's diary records Thomas Bott paying him £5 for painting some tiles.

Charles Baldwyn entered a lot of his watercolour work into competitions and won many prizes from national magazines. His work was of sufficient quality that he went on to have several exhibitions at the Royal Academy.

Although famous for his renditions of swans and other birds, Baldwyn's repertoire was broad and he could paint subject matters as diverse as rabbits, dogs, cattle, foxes, bats and even tigers with similar degrees of excellence.

He was a sociable character and great friends with William Hawkins. He was a member of the works cycling club and frequently held musical evenings in his house in Arboretum Road. His father was a piano tuner and harpist.

Charles left the factory in 1904 to work as a freelance watercolourist employing an agent to sell his paintings for him. He died in 1943.

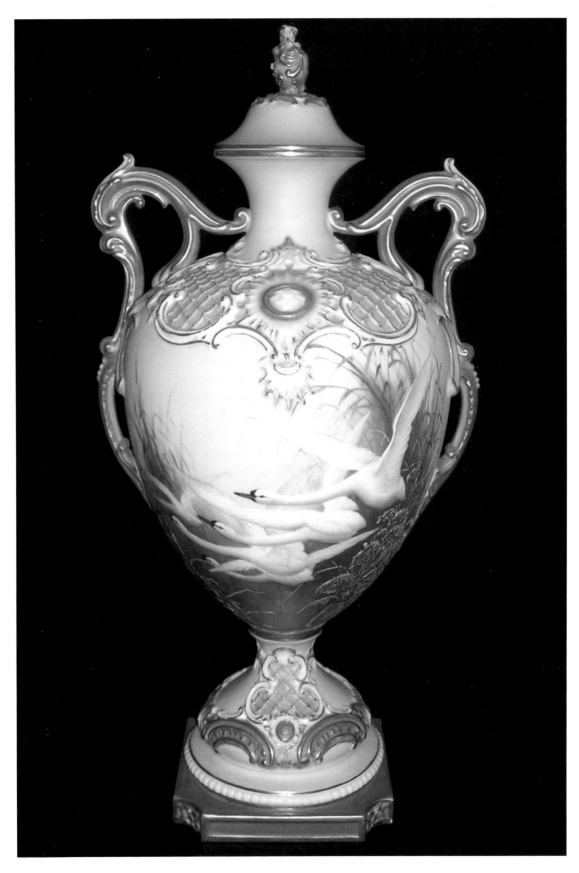

A magnificent flying swans vase by Charles Baldwyn,
dated 1901, shape 2010, standing 42cm high.

A superb flying swans plate signed C. Baldwyn, dated 1901, 25cm wide.

A very rare and truly outstanding pair of vases signed C. Baldwyn,
dated 1900, shape number 2007, standing 42cm high.

A very unusual pot-pourri signed C. Baldwyn painted with seagulls
flying around cliff tops, dated 1906, shape 1515, 28cm high.

A very rare pot-pourri painted with rabbits signed CHC Baldwyn,
dated 1900, shape 1515, 20cm high.

A Charles Baldwyn vase beautifully painted with four flying swans,
dated 1891, shape number 1618, 27cm high.

A large exhibition quality plaque signed CHC Baldwyn,
painted with swimming swans, dated 1901, 30cm diameter.

A very well painted pot-pourri signed C. Baldwyn,
dated 1899, shape 1515, 20cm high.

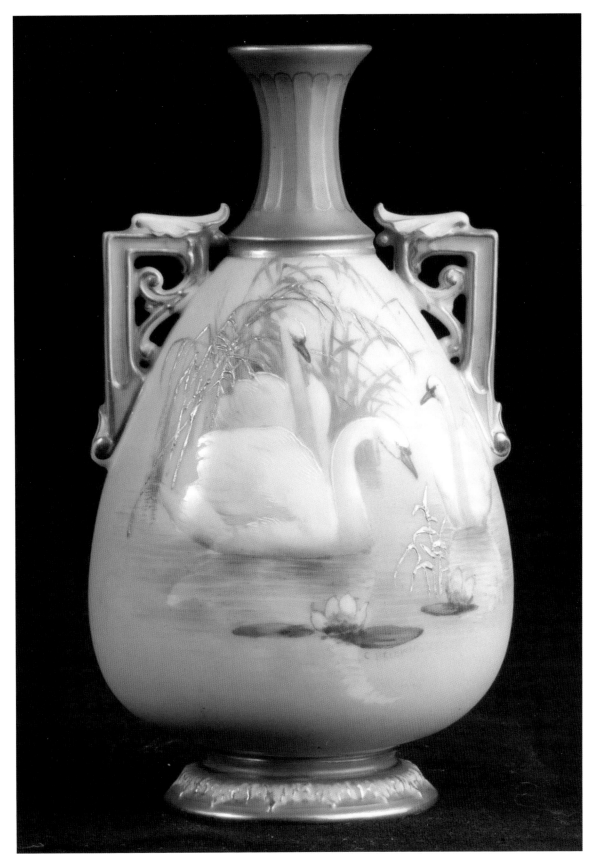

A little rarer than flying swans are swimming swans,
signed C. Baldwyn, dated 1899, shape 1539, 17cm high.

A fine pair of vases painted and signed C. Baldwyn,
dated 1901, shape 1927, 23cm high.

An exquisite pair of vases signed CHC. Baldwyn,
dated 1899, shape 1970, 29cm high.

An excellent vase painted with songbirds amongst thistles,
signed C. Baldwyn, dated 1899, shape 2010, standing 42cm high.

A finely painted vase depicting British birds on thistles,
signed C. Baldwyn, dated 1900, shape 1835, 33cm high.

A fine flying swans vase by C. Baldwyn,
dated 1902, shape number 1572, standing 27cm high.

A very good vase painted with doves, signed C. Baldwyn,
dated 1903, shape 2307, 29cm high.

A blush ewer painted with doves outside a country manor,
signed C. Baldwyn, dated 1906, shape 2055, standing 30cm high.

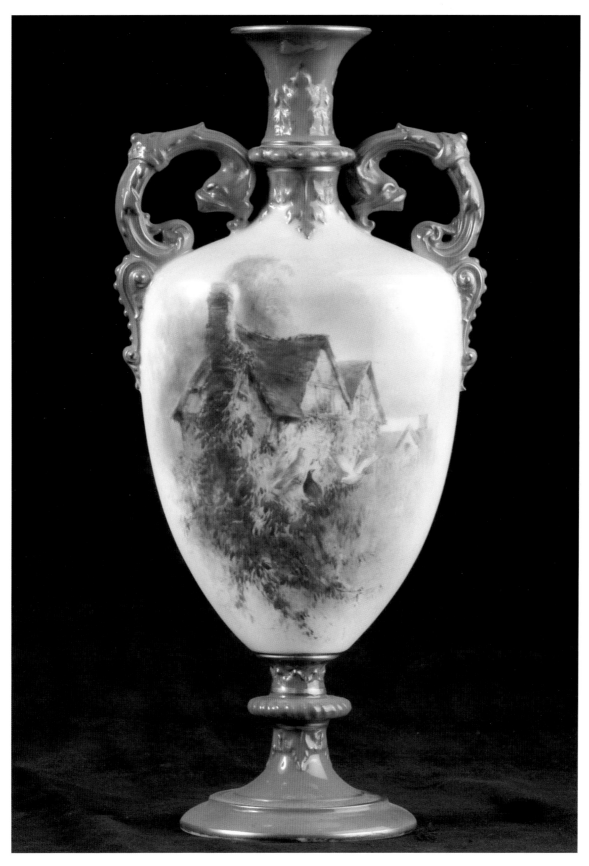

A vase painted with a country manor house with doves perched in the garden,
signed C. Baldwyn, dated 1904, shape 2337, 30cm high.

John Stinton (Junior)

BORN IN 1854, John Stinton was the eldest son of John Stinton senior and started painting at the Worcester Grainger factory in 1889 at the age of 35. After the take over of Grainger's in 1902, he moved across to the Royal Worcester factory with his younger brother James.

John is mostly known for his wonderful renditions of Highland cattle in scenic hillside settings (although it is said that he never once set foot over the Scottish border). He was also able to paint English cattle and was a skilled landscape artist, producing many plate centres depicting famous British castles.

Handed down through the Stinton dynasty was the tradition of mixing oil of cloves with the paint to stop it drying out too quickly. The studio was always filled with the strong smell of cloves.

John Stinton is justifiably a highly collected 'name' and is thought by many to be one of the finest ceramic and watercolour landscape artists of all time. He retired in 1938.

A genial old man, he was an inveterate smoker, never painting without his pipe going all the while. Outside the workplace, John was a keen gardener and a very practical man. He kept a heated glasshouse where he grew and cured the pipe tobacco that he smoked incessantly. It obviously did him no great harm as he lived to the ripe old age of 102, dying in 1956.

An impressive bough pot painted with Highland cattle, signed J. Stinton,
dated 1919, shape 1428, 33cm high.

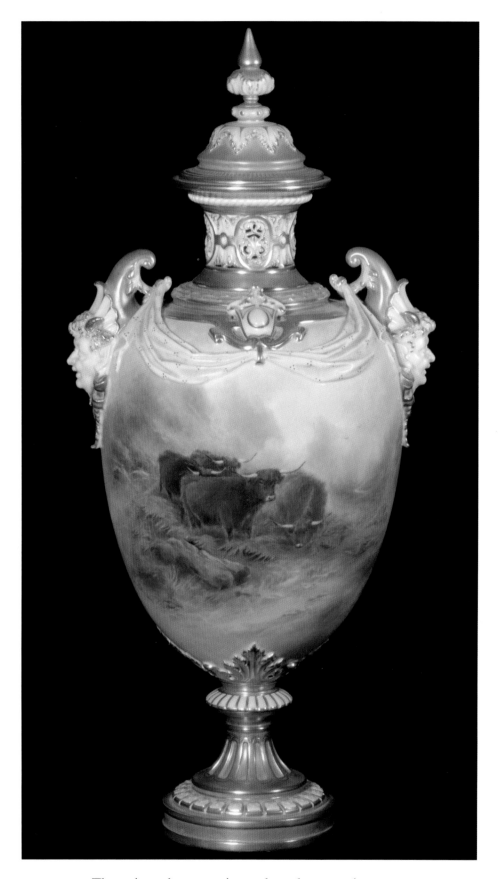

The pair to the vase pictured on the opposite page.

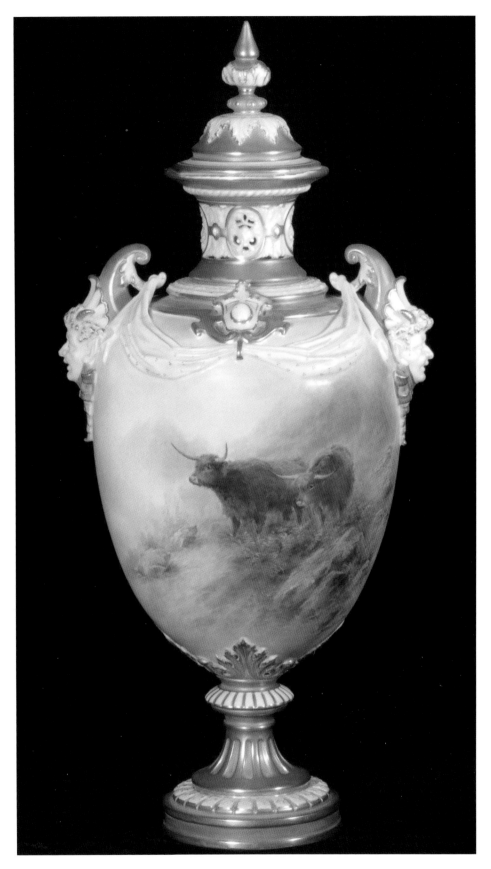

An impressive urn shaped vase signed J. Stinton,
dated 1904, shape number 1407, 50cm high.

A magnificent pair of cattle vases signed John Stinton, dated 1923,
shape 2007, standing 57cm high.

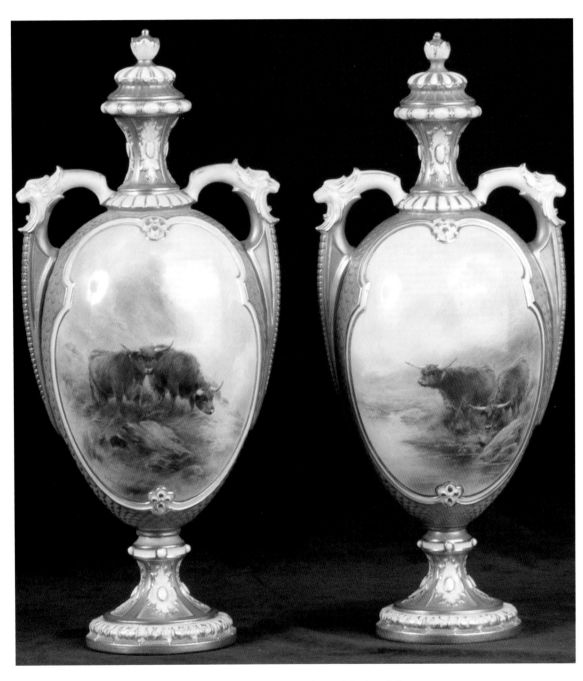

A superb pair of vases signed John Stinton,
dated 1912, shape 2330, 36cm high.

A impressive jardinière painted all around by John Stinton,
dated 1923, shape number H256, standing 31cm high.

A superbly painted vase signed J. Stinton,
depicting Highland cattle in the Scottish Highlands,
dated 1909, shape 2336, standing 37cm high.

An excellent pair of Highland cattle vases signed John Stinton,
dated 1905, shape 2425, standing 35cm.

An exceptional pair of vases painted with Highland cattle signed John Stinton, dated 1925, shape H248, standing 40cm high.

A cobalt blue Highland cattle vase signed J. Stinton,
dated 1912, shape 1969, 52cm high.

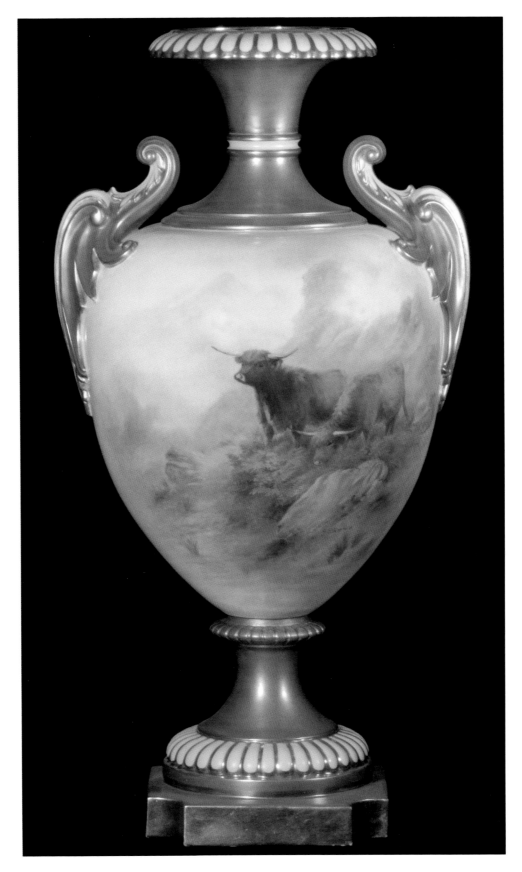

A large vase signed J. Stinton, painted with the classic Scottish
Highland cattle scene, dated 1916, shape 1969, 56cm high.

An excellent vase painted with English cattle, signed J. Stinton,
dated 1905, shape number 2151, 28cm high.

A magnificent pair of ewers finely painted by John Stinton,
dated 1921, shape 1309, standing 41cm high.

A magnificent bough pot painted with Highland cattle, signed John Stinton, dated 1909, shape 1428, standing 36cm high.

A magnificent jardinière painted all around by John Stinton,
dated 1910, shape H157, 22cm high.

A fine pair of plaques painted by John Stinton,
dated 1920, size 23cm x 15cm.

You won't get better painting than this pair of John Stinton cattle vases,
dated 1924, shape 2510, standing 28cm high.

A superb rose jar painted with Highland cattle,
signed J. Stinton, dated 1925, shape 2048, 35cm high.

An excellent painting of Highland cattle on this jardinière,
signed J. Stinton, dated 1911, shape 1523, standing 23cm high.

Royal Worcester fruit painters of the 1920s

QUALITY FRUIT PAINTING on vases and tableware is a theme that has run strongly throughout the history of Royal Worcester and at no time was it more eminent than with the talented and exciting group of painters assembled in the 1920s.

The likes of Reginald Austin and his brother Walter Austin, Harry Ayrton, William Bagnall, William Bee, John Freeman, Thomas Lockyer, George Moseley, Horace Price, William Ricketts, Richard Sebright, Albert Shuck, Edward Townsend and Charlie Twilton provided a pool of extraordinary talent under the foremanship of the renowned William Hawkins that could not be matched at any other porcelain works in the country.

The 1920s started with great enthusiasm at Royal Worcester with post war euphoria running riot, but hard times were to follow swiftly and many of the fine body of 'name' painters were forced into finding alternative sources of income and in some cases, alternative means of employment. The 1920s were, in many respects, the last great era of the ceramic art form.

Reginald Harry Austin

BORN IN 1890, Reginald Austin, better known as Harry, studied art at Worcester College. He specialised in fruit painting, along with flowers (particularly Australian wild flowers) and birds - the latter perhaps becoming his best known subjects. He stayed at Royal Worcester throughout the 1920s, supplementing his income by selling watercolours locally, but left in 1930 during the height of the depression to do freelance work where he could earn more money. He later went to work in the Potteries where he painted a service for the birth of Princess Margaret before returning to the city of Worcester (but not the Royal Worcester factory). He died in 1955.

Walter Harold Austin

WALTER AUSTIN WAS the brother of Harry and was one year younger. Like Harry, he won several medals for his drawings of plants including the King's Prize and these were to be his major area of excellence. He was, however, a fine fruit painter and produced many pieces during his stay at Royal Worcester. Like his brother, he produced many watercolours as a sideline to boost his earnings during the difficult times and finally left the Royal Worcester factory in 1930. He worked for some years as a painter of flowers on furniture, a very popular fashion at the time. He lived until 1971 and it is said that he never once worked during the month of September when he would follow his love of fishing in Scotland and Ireland.

Harry (Tim) Ayrton

HARRY AYRTON (1905 -1976) started at the Royal Worcester factory in 1920 where he stayed until his retirement in 1970. He was a member of the group of apprentices that became known as the 'Terrible Seven' - in the most playful and harmless of manner, they would terrorise the other Royal Worcester workers and 'skive off' to play football or cricket whenever the opportunity arose - often in inappropriate places! He was also a very keen member of the works cycling club and participated in many of their outings and races. Although trained to paint many different subjects, Harry was most skilful at fruit painting and this was his major topic throughout the 1920s.

William Bagnall

WILLIAM BAGNALL WAS another of the 'Terrible Seven' apprentices. He started at Royal Worcester in 1918 and became a fine fruit painter and a master of still life subjects. William did not fare as well as some of the others during the hard times ahead, eventually leaving in the early 1930s to take over a fish and chip shop in Guildford. Like all the others in this list, his work is highly regarded and much sought after.

William Bee

YET ANOTHER OF the 'Terrible Seven' that livened up the Royal Worcester factory at this time, William Bee was a great fruit painter whose talents were wasted by the severe depression that swept the world. He left in 1932 and nothing significant is known about his later life. He died in 1976.

John Freeman

JOHN FREEMAN WAS born in 1911 and joined the Royal Worcester factory in 1925 just when the major problems were starting. He became an extremely talented fruit painter and was probably the most prolific of all the fruit painters of his time. He stayed at the Royal Worcester factory throughout his long working life and became the senior fruit painter in the men's painting room. John Freeman was known amongst his colleagues as 'The Fruit Machine' because of the speed at which he could turn out fruit painted plates.

Thomas Lockyer

THOMAS LOCKYER WORKED at the Royal Worcester factory from before the beginning of the First World War as a specialist fruit painter. He had his own style of painting dessert fruits against a mossy background that was mouth-wateringly real. He left the factory temporarily to serve in the armed forces during the war where he was wounded and left with a permanent limp. He stayed at the Royal Worcester factory, producing his stunning fruit paintings until his death in 1935. The work of Thomas Lockyer is very collectable.

George Moseley

GEORGE MOSELEY WAS another of the 'Terrible Seven' apprentices at the factory. He started in 1919 and became an adept, if slightly less well known, painter of fruit and small birds. Small pieces may simply bear the monogram "GM". He stayed at the Royal Worcester factory until 1939 when he left to join the army. He died in 1973.

Horace Price

BORN IN 1898, Horace Price started work at the Royal Worcester factory in 1912 and stayed there throughout his working life. He was a keen and well respected fruit painter that could also turn his hand to flowers in both the general Royal Worcester and the Hadley styles. He served in the First World War where he lost a finger on his right hand but this seemed to make no difference to his work and he was greatly admired by the factory management. Horace Price later became foreman of all the apprentice painters and died in 1965.

William Ricketts

WILLIAM RICKETTS (1862 - 1938) worked at the Royal Worcester factory from around 1877 until the early 1930s. He was a skilled painter of flowers but was best known for his fruit painting. He would usually paint this as a composition including a vase or other ornament and developed his own style using oils that broke up the paints to provide a unique 'mottled' background to his work. William Ricketts was also a skilled watercolourist and his work was exhibited at the Royal Academy. He was one of the most highly regarded of the Royal Worcester fruit painters of his time.

Richard Sebright

RICHARD SEBRIGHT IS possibly the most highly regarded fruit painter of all time. He worked at the Royal Worcester factory painting fruits for a total of fifty six years and during all of that time was never able to make a decent living from it. Painters were paid per finished piece so the more they produced the more they earned. Sebright was so painstaking in his work and so determined that each piece would be the best that he could produce, he was never able to work fast enough to earn as much money as the others did. It is said that he was a very religious man who never married. His religion and work were paramount to him and the level of his earnings was of only minor consequence.

Albert Shuck

ALBERT SHUCK (1880 - 1961) painted fruit and flowers at Royal Worcester throughout the 1920s. He was regarded as a very shy and reserved man and only became animated when discussing his favourite subject of painting. He was a skilled watercolourist and well liked by his fellow workers.

Edward (Ted) Townsend

ONE OF THE 'Terrible Seven', Edward Townsend started at the Royal Worcester factory in 1918 and stayed there until he retired in 1971. He loved painting fruit but was also skilled in many other areas. He became assistant foreman to Harry Davis and then took over his role in 1954 when Davis retired.

Charlie Twilton

ANOTHER OF THE 'Terrible Seven', Charlie Twilton started his apprenticeship at Royal Worcester in 1918. Although he was a fine fruit painter, he was always much too slow and left the factory during the depression to become a spray painter of cars!

William Hawkins

LEFT UNTIL LAST, William Hawkins was the foreman of the men's painting room throughout most of the 1920s until his retirement in 1928 and is one of the most respected painters to have worked at Royal Worcester. Although he was not renowned for his fruit paintings, he was certainly more than competent. His real love and best work were in the area of portraits and still life subjects. Having put up with the antics of the 'Terrible Seven' apprentices during his later years, it seems churlish to leave him out of the section on fruit painters.

A boat shaped pedestal bowl painted with fruit, signed E. Townsend,
dated 1937, shape H254, 35cm long.

A very well painted fruit vase signed R. Sebright, dated 1933,
shape 2713, standing 20cm high.

An excellent vase painted with fruit, signed W. Ricketts,
dated 1923, shape number 1572, standing 27cm high.

A good pot-pourri painted with fruit, signed J. Freeman,
dated 1941, shape 2048, standing 35cm high.

A fine cased set of coffee cans and saucers painted by various artists,
dated 1929.

A pair of scalloped edge fruit plates,
signed T. Lockyer, size 22cm, dated 1929/1930.

A pair of scalloped edge fruit plates,
signed R. Sebright, size 22cm, dated 1940/1941.

A pair of scalloped edge fruit plates,
signed H. Price, size 22cm, dated 1938.

A pair of scalloped edge fruit plates,
signed F. Roberts, size 22cm, dated 1919/1912.

A pair of scalloped edge fruit plates,
signed H. Price, size 22cm, dated 1935.

A pair of scalloped edge fruit plates,
signed H. Price, size 22cm, dated 1929.

George Owen

ONE OF THE true enigmas of porcelain manufacture, George Owen was a craftsman without peer. He became a master of reticulation - the painstaking and difficult art of piercing porcelain with intricate patterns of holes.

George Owen was born in 1845 and worked in the Royal Worcester factory during the lean years of the 1880s and 1890s. Work was hard to come by and many artists and craftsmen were forced to find other ways to supplement their earnings. Some turned their skills to other areas and painted on canvas, paper or wood for private sale.

In an effort to develop new skills, George began to experiment with incredibly fine patterned piercing of the porcelain in order to produce works with an appearance of lace work (also known as reticulation). Reticulated work was not new - many factories produced their own examples and relatively large amounts of finely pierced vases were being produced in Worcester at this time by the Grainger factory. However, despite being self taught, the quality of George Owen's work was breathtaking and put him in a league of his own.

Exactly how he produced these vases will never be known with certainty. In those days, keeping your 'tricks of the trade' secret might have meant the difference between being employed or being out of work. There are many examples of workers of the times being the only people who knew how to do their job or what the recipe was for their particular part of the manufacturing process. It seems a strange situation today, but understandable in those days when there was no social security and workers did what they could to protect their living. George didn't even teach his own son the art of reticulation.

He would only work alone and behind locked doors. If anyone wanted to come in, they would have to wait until he had hidden his work and tools away before the door was opened. He was very strict about this and it made no difference who was at the door. Director or apprentice, they would have to wait until he was ready. Such secrecy prevented imitation, allowing George's extraordinary ability to be sought after, even during periods of downturn within the industry. Even more importantly, it also meant that his concentration was not disturbed.

He had the uncanny ability to take a complete vase, without moulding or patterns and as he slowly revolved it on a turntable, he would cut hole after hole, row after row perfectly into place (often varying the size of each row to graduate the holes and enhance the effect). The detail and incredible regularity of the piercing was so fine and intricate, that it is quite unbelievable and almost impossible to comprehend that the work was done by human hands.

George worked with vases that were cast specifically for him by his son and were extremely thin walled. This made it possible for him to pierce the holes with more precision but it also made the vases more fragile. He would cut the small holes with a sharp, oil covered knife and would always have just the right amount of space left for the last hole or the last row - no doubt a skill that was helped considerably by being ambidextrous.

He could cut holes from either inside or outside the piece, with either hand. One problem was the control of the small pieces he cut out. If it was possible to work from within the vase then the cut outs would fall on the outside. However, if he was working from the outside, then the pieces may fall inside the vase, dry and become irretrievable. A pot with a pile of dried 'off cuts' inside would not be acceptable to anyone. It is said that he dipped his knives in oil to make the clay stick to the blade and come away with the knife.

Making these vases was a long term commitment. Large and complicated pieces might take months to produce. They could only be worked on during their 'green stage', while the clay was firm enough to hold its shape but still wet enough to work. This stage would only last a few minutes - time only to do a few dozen holes, especially during the Summer months when the workshops would become unbearably warm. Then the vase would become too dry and brittle to work on and would have to be put back into a 'wet-box' - a metal lined box containing wet cloths - until the clay absorbed the moisture from the atmosphere and became workable again.

He had a good supply of such boxes and had to work on a lot of different pieces at the same time - doing a small amount and then putting it back in the wet box and working on another. Swapping from piece to piece, it must have been difficult to remember what pattern he was planning to apply to that particular piece. Usually the reticulation covered almost the entire vase and it seems amazing that it didn't collapse. Even the handles and lids were pierced.

Not only was the process time consuming, the work on each piece would be spread over several months. Right up to the end, there was no certainty that it would be successful. In the kiln, anything could go wrong with these fragile pieces and they could end up broken or distorted.

Some pieces were made with only partial reticulation and the rest of the body painted with flowers, usually by Harry Chair or occasionally Ernest Phillips.

In keeping with the nature of George's work, to finish off the pieces, they were embellished with extremely fine and intricate gilding - the final product being a work of extraordinary beauty and craftsmanship.

Mistakes were easy to make. One small slip of the knife would join two holes together and the vase would be ruined. Even if he managed to go through the entire process without a slip, the delicate structure between the holes could split during the firing stage and again the piece would be spoilt. No-one knows what his success or failure rate was, but it was obviously high enough for him to consider it worth doing. It is so easy to imagine the knife slipping, or a little too much pressure being applied to the eggshell like body, that he must have suffered many disappointments.

George must have been a man of great patience and solitude and he kept very much to himself. The fact that he needed to operate skilfully and quickly, coupled with the knowledge that a momentary lapse in concentration could ruin his work reveals the cool composure and immense ability of the man.

The factory was very proud of George's achievements and supported him in his endeavours. But these were hard times and they could only afford to pay him for completed pieces and not for his time if the work was not successfully finished for some reason. A lot of the work was done in his spare time, or whilst waiting for official work orders to come in.

His work gave Royal Worcester extra variety in their product range and was featured prominently in the company's worldwide exhibitions - the Chicago World Fair in 1893 and The Franco-British Exhibition in 1908 in particular.

George's work is usually signed with 'G. Owen' being scratched, or incised, into the raw clay usually on the base of the piece. Sometimes he wrote his name on in gilt. As signing their work only became a common practice at Royal Worcester after 1900, it is reasonable to assume that many of his earlier pieces aren't signed. However, because George did a lot of work in his own time, the general rules of the factory may not have applied to the same degree.

Owing to the unique nature and beauty of George's work, his pieces are very collectable and highly sought after. Their fragility means that many have not survived the ravages of time and their value is increasing steadily.

With the death of George Owen in 1917, the world lost one of the truly unique and supremely talented craftsmen. His workmanship was incredible - the like of which has never been seen before or since. If it didn't already exist, you would think it couldn't be done. His secrets died with him. However, he lives on in the form of his beautiful pieces - holding pride of place in collections around the world.

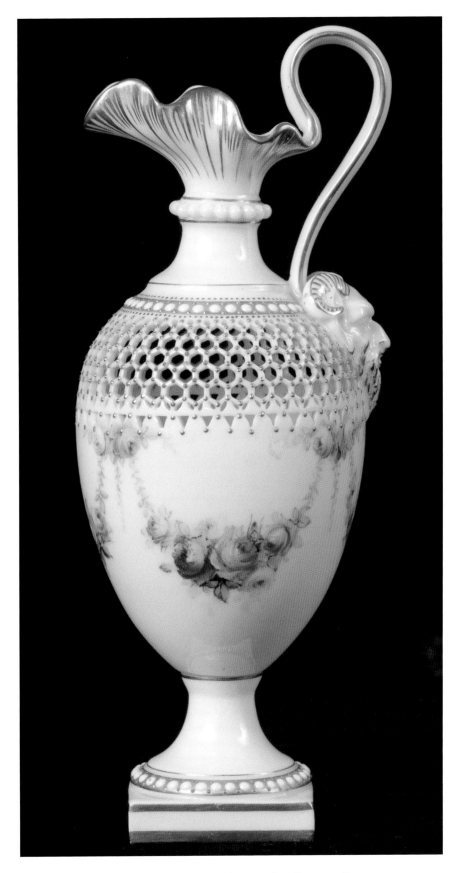

An excellent reticulated ewer by George Owen,
dated 1904, shape 1144, 17cm high.
The flower decoration is by Harry Chair.

Two photos to show the detail of the extraordinary workmanship in the vase
pictured on the opposite page. The lower picture shows a
different pattern in the reticulated medallion on the back of the vase.

A fine example of George Owen's work,
showing his reticulating skills at their very best,
dated 1894, shape 1552, 23cm high.

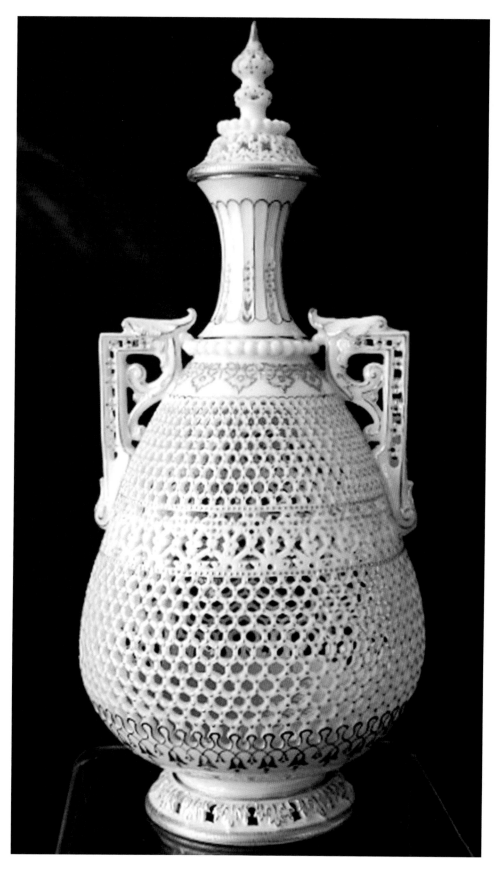

An outstanding vase by George Owen, dated 1896,
shape 1539, standing 20cm high.

An excellent vase by George Owen, dated 1917,
shape 2363, 21cm high.

A very decorative reticulated slipper by George Owen,
dated 1907, shape 763, 16cm long.

A fine reticulated trinket box by George Owen,
dated 1912, shape 2416, 10cm high.

A very rare jewelled hand and reticulated trumpet vase by
George Owen, dated 1894, shape 36, 18cm high.

A finely reticulated tea pot by George Owen,
dated 1898, standing 12cm high.

A very fine and rare set of four reticulated cups and saucers
by George Owen, dated 1887.

William Hawkins

BORN IN 1858, William Hawkins painted at Royal Worcester from the age of 16 in 1874 until he retired in 1928. For 47 years he was foreman of the male painting department, producing training aids and supervising the teaching of the young apprentices while still continuing to do his own work. He must be regarded as one of the most highly prized of all the Royal Worcester painters. As foreman over an exceptionally talented group of artists during these golden years, his place in the history of Royal Worcester cannot be undervalued.

William was a very adept painter of portrait and figure studies, both original compositions and also in imitation of the 'masters'. He was noted for his many still life, fruit and floral subjects, often in room settings.

His early work may be initialled 'WAH' before the use of full signatures became common in about 1900.

William was always strongly involved with the welfare and well-being of the factory and its workforce. He was a member of the Education and Entertainments Committee, captain of the works cycling club and was obviously liked by the workforce and the company managers.

He was considered by all to be a true gentleman and passed away in 1930.

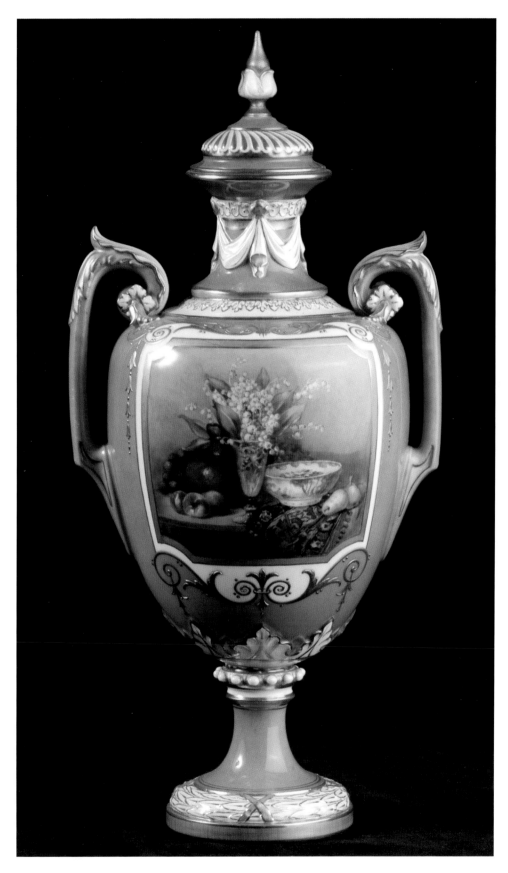

A glorious Rose du Barry pink vase painted with a still life,
signed W. Hawkins, dated 1914, shape 1482, 38cm high.

These pictures show the exceptional raised gilding work on the vase
pictured opposite - this is the work of master gilder Albert Glover.

A impressive exhibition cobalt blue vase, signed W. Hawkins,
dated 1899, shape 1969, standing 52cm high.

A good still life vase, signed W. Hawkins,
dated 1920, shape 2354, 36cm high.

A fine cobalt blue vase painted with a still life,
signed W. Hawkins, dated 1910, shape 2432, 28cm high.

Here's an extremely rare subject - a pair of leopard cubs,
signed W. A. Hawkins, dated 1925, 25cm diameter.

A large cobalt blue vase, signed W. Hawkins,
dated 1903, shape 1969, standing 52cm high.

A cobalt blue vase with the front panel painted with strawberries by
W. Hawkins, dated 1898, shape 1937, standing 25cm high.

A very rare plaque by W. Hawkins, after the painting by Thomas Gainsborough
entitled "The Blue Boy" (1770), dated 1925, 23cm x 15cm.
The original work is in the Huntington Gallery in California.

Richard Sebright

BORN IN 1868, Richard Sebright worked as an artist at the Royal Worcester factory for a total of fifty six years until he retired in the late 1940s.

He was a very quality conscious and dedicated man and was regarded by many, including his fellow workers, as being the finest fruit painter of all time.

He painted from life and would spend much of his free time making water colours of in-season fruit so that he could copy them later for his ceramic work.

There can be no doubt about the sheer quality and professionalism of his work, but in some ways it could be said that he took it to extremes. His work was so painfully slow and meticulous that he was never able to make a decent living. Painters at this time were paid on a piece rate, so much per finished and approved painting, and he flatly refused to speed up or cut corners to increase his earnings. Richard was also a fine painter of flowers and produced several watercolours which were exhibited at the Royal Academy.

It is said that he lived an obsessional life with his spinster sister in Worcester. He was a devoutly religious man and thought only about his fruit painting and religion. In the later stages of his life, the religion became a mania and he would rant and rave at the factory about the (imagined) shameless conduct of his fellow workers. He passed away in 1951.

Please view pages 74 and 79 for other fine examples of Sebright's work.

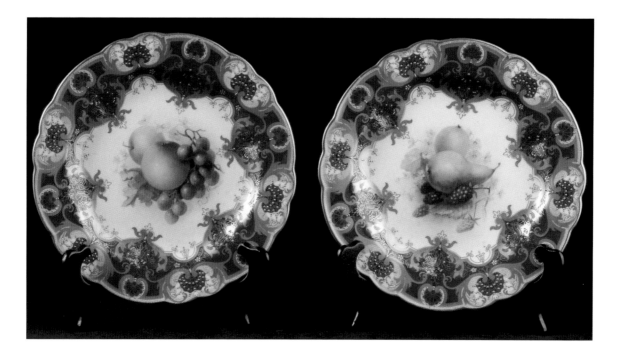

Painted and signed R. Sebright, cobalt blue finish,
dated 1914, superb shape 2401, 28cm high.

A pair of urn shaped vases painted with fruit in a basket, signed R. Sebright,
dated 1909, shape 2448, 21cm high.

An excellent cobalt blue vase painted with fruit, signed R. Sebright,
dated 1901, shape 1572, 27cm high.

A fine cobalt blue vase, signed R. Sebright,
dated 1913, shape 2336, standing 35cm high.

Another superb vase painted with fruit by R. Sebright,
dated 1930, shape 2048, standing 25cm high.

A very impressive plate with the centre painted with fruit,
signed R. Sebright, dated 1920, 27cm wide.

A pair of cobalt blue vases painted with still life fruit,
signed R. Sebright, dated 1933, shape 2305, 28cm high.

Walter Powell

WALTER POWELL STARTED at the Hadley factory in Worcester in 1900 when they first started to employ quality freehand painters. He was a fine craftsman, known for his flowers and foreign birds, especially storks and flamingos.

When the Hadley factory was taken over by Royal Worcester in 1905, he moved across to their paint shop and stayed there, doing the same bird studies, until he left to fight in the First World War.

He survived the war but did not return to England, staying in France with a girl he met. There is some evidence to suggest that he painted for the Sèvres factory in the 1920s.

He was a wonderful artist, with very atmospheric paintings that are highly thought of and very sought after, although his work is rare. There are many fine watercolours of similar subject matter that are also highly collectable.

An excellent jardinière painted with peacocks, signed W. Powell,
dated 1905, shape H191, 16cm high.

A magnificent rose jar painted by W. Powell with flamingos in a misty
lake setting, dated 1910, shape 2048, 30cm high.

A crisp and colourful vase painted with storks in an oasis setting,
signed W. Powell, dated 1912, shape G42, standing 23cm high.

A superbly shaped vase painted by W. Powell with storks
in a lagoon setting, dated 1903, shape F100, 38cm high.

A good vase painted by W. Powell with storks in an oasis,
dated 1912, shape 1410, 29cm high.

A good peacock vase, signed W. Powell,
dated 1908, shape number 2430, 36cm high.

A very decorative vase painted with storks in an oasis,
signed W. Powell, dated 1911, shape 2151, 28cm high.

A very colourful jardinière painted with irises, signed W. Powell,
dated 1912, shape H256, standing 31cm high.

Harry Stinton

Another of the renowned Stinton family, Harry was the son of John Junior and the nephew of James. Born in 1883, Harry started at the Royal Worcester factory in 1896 and studied under his father to produce the same Highland cattle scenes, though with a palette that tended more towards purple.

Although he was an extremely talented artist, whilst his father was alive, Harry's work was confined to the smaller and lower-paid pieces. He also had a broad repertoire and could turn his hand to painting fruit, birds and even sheep. A great exhibitor, Harry won several medals from the National Art School and went on to become a greatly respected watercolourist covering landscapes and cattle subjects similar to those he depicted on porcelain.

He was a keen chess player and fisherman and would spend much of his spare time out with Harry Davis on the banks of the River Severn.

Towards his latter years, Harry's eyesight began to deteriorate and his style of painting changed recognizably, with the cattle becoming less clearly defined and assuming a stipple-painted Impressionistic style.

Harry retired in 1963 after 67 years at the factory and died in 1968.

A pair of Highland cattle vases signed H. Stinton,
dated 1917, shape 2049, standing 25cm high.

A good pair of vases painted by Harry Stinton,
dated 1915, shape number H307, 21cm high.

Here's a different subject - a stag and deer in a wood clearing,
signed H. Stinton, dated 1926, shape H169, standing 17cm high.

A fine pair of cattle vases signed H. Stinton, dated 1918, shape 1858, standing 33cm high, which is very large for a piece of Harry Stinton's work.

A superbly painted rose jar by Harry Stinton,
dated 1920, shape number 2048, standing 25cm high.

Frank Roberts

FRANK ROBERTS WAS born in 1857 and started work at the Royal Worcester factory in 1872. He was an exceptional painter of fruit in the expected Worcester style but was also noted for his superb renditions of flowers (particularly orchids) and would sometimes do raised gold work.

He was a man noted for being very insular and with strong religious convictions. In later days, many of his pieces were used in the training of new apprentices.

Frank stayed with the Royal Worcester factory until just before he died in 1920.

His work should not be confused with the later artist, William Roberts, who was also noted for his fruit paintings. The difference lies in the date as William Roberts did not start at the factory until 1930.

Please see page 81 for examples of the fruit painting of Frank Roberts.

A superb vase painted with roses signed F. Roberts,
dated 1906, shape number 1847, 42cm high.

A truly magnificent vase painted with peony roses,
signed F. Roberts, dated 1902, shape 2007, standing 57cm high.

The peony rose vase opposite, standing on a Royal Worcester pedestal
painted by George Cole, total height 107cm.

An exceptional pair of cobalt blue vases painted with still life fruit,
signed F. Roberts, dated 1919, shape 1969, size 50cm.

A lovely orchid campana vase painted by Frank Roberts,
dated 1900, shape number 1868, 13cm high.

James (Jas) Stinton

BORN IN 1870, James Stinton was the younger brother of John Stinton (junior). He started with the Grainger factory and moved to the Royal Worcester works when Grainger's was taken over in 1902.

James is particularly well known for his fine paintings of game birds depicted in their natural setting, particularly pheasants and grouse. Over the years, he painted a large number of ornamental vases, plate centres and tea sets.

As his elder brother's signature was also 'J. Stinton', James elected to sign his paintings as 'Jas Stinton' to distinguish his work from that of his brother.

James is also well known for his watercolours, mostly of the same subjects he painted on porcelain.

For many years, James would paint a Royal Worcester plate and send it to his brother in America for a birthday or Christmas gift.

John, Harry and James Stinton always used to arrive together at the factory in the morning, proceeding to the painting room in that order. Their fellow workers would refer to them as 'The Holy Trinity".

James retired in 1951 at the age of 81 and died in 1961.

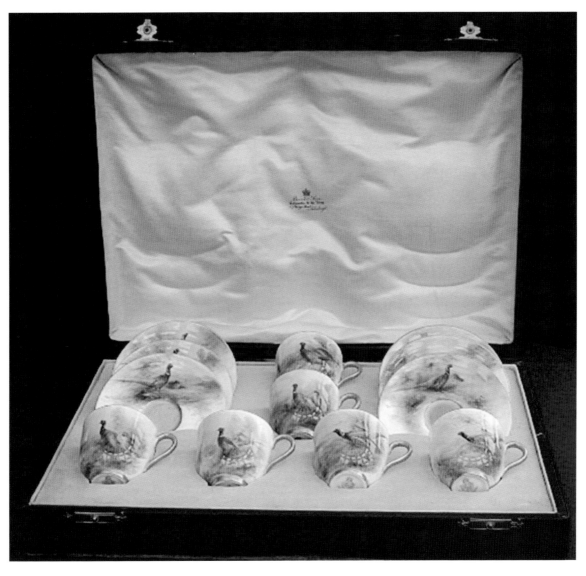

A fine set of cups and saucers all painted with cock and hen pheasants,
signed Jas Stinton, dated 1925.

A fine pot-pourri painted with golden pheasants, signed Jas Stinton,
dated 1905, shape number 1515, 21cm high.

A superbly painted vase signed Jas Stinton,
dated 1914, shape number G42, 23cm high.

A good vase painted with pheasants by Jas Stinton,
dated 1912, shape 2032, 28cm high.

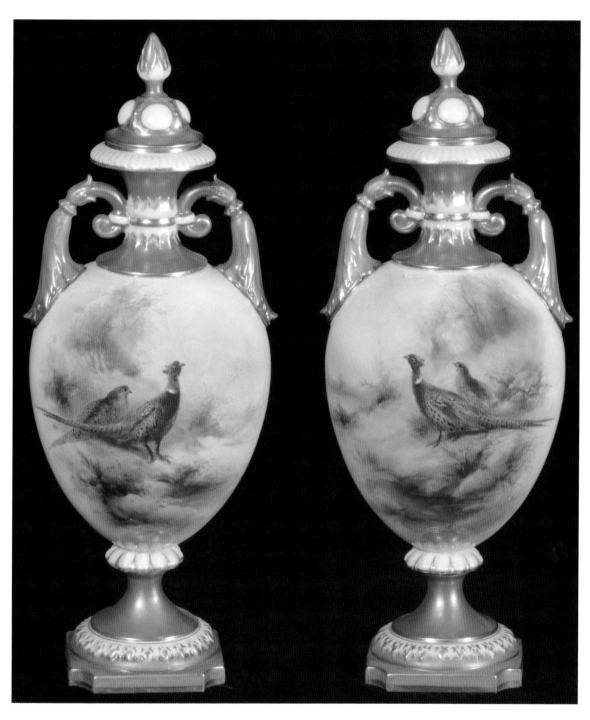

A fine pair of vases signed Jas Stinton,
dated 1912, shape number 2443, 28cm high.

William Powell

BORN IN 1878, William Powell started at the Royal Worcester factory in 1900 and stayed until 1950.

William was a totally devoted painter of British birds and flowers, painting them with great detail and accuracy.

He would spend all his spare time out in the country side with his camera taking pictures for further study.

William was called, in those days at least, a hunchback and dwarf. He was a perpetually cheerful man who was well liked and respected by his fellow workers and by the public who would see him painting during the conducted tours through the factory.

Three milk jugs painted by William Powell, various dates in the 1930s,
size around 10cm.

The Goldfinch,
signed W. Powell,
dated 1931.

The Kingfisher,
signed W. Powell,
dated 1931.

The Bullfinch,
signed W. Powell,
dated 1931.

The Wren,
signed W. Powell,
dated 1931.

The Grey Tit,
signed W. Powell,
dated 1931.

The Redstart,
signed W. Powell,
dated 1931.

Edward Salter

BORN IN 1860, Edward (Ted) Salter worked as a highly skilled artist at the Royal Worcester works from 1876 until his death in 1902.

He was a brilliant landscape artist and he was chosen to illustrate the Championship Cup for the factory's own cycling club in 1893 with a painting of Tewksbury Bridge.

A keen angler, Salter not only passed on his talents to his apprentice, Harry Davis, but also a love of fishing. He would often take Harry on a fishing trip and get him to study and paint the fish he caught.

Salter is probably best known as a painter of fish in natural settings and many plate centres are known to have been painted by him. Signed pieces by Salter are extremely rare however, as signing their work only became common practice at Royal Worcester a short while before his death.

He is believed to have committed suicide, for an unknown reason, and his death greatly upset his student and friend, Harry Davis.

A beautifully painted pair of plates by E. Salter, dated 1902.
This pair come from an important set of plates as it represented the last work of Salter and also the first official work of Harry Davis, who was released early from his apprenticeship to complete the set upon the untimely death of Salter.

A superb jardinière painted with a shipwreck on rough seas,
signed E. Salter, dated 1899, shape 1176, 24cm high.

Loving cup
– Harry Davis, George Cole and Harry Chair

Here is a unique piece – a three handled loving cup with three different cartouches painted by three different artists.

The first panel is painted with a country scene signed H. Davis.
The second panel is painted with fruit signed G. Cole.
The third panel is painted with flowers signed H. Chair..

It is dated 1910, shape number 2217, standing 23cm high.

Walter Sedgley

WALTER SEDGLEY WORKED at the Royal Worcester factory from 1889 until 1929.

He was regarded by his colleagues as the finest of the Hadley rose style painters and was also noted for his rendering of golden pheasants, flowers and general landscape work. His other speciality depicted colourful renditions of Italian lakeside garden scenes.

Walter was one of the senior painters and many apprentices learnt their craft under his tutorage.

As with several other of the Worcester artists, Walter also did some of the colouring in of pre-printed designs but would never sign his own name to these. He used the signatures 'Seeley' and 'J Walters' for these pieces.

He died shortly after his retirement from tuberculosis.

A beautiful rose jardinière signed W. Sedgley,
dated 1911, shape H295, 19cm high.

A very decorative pair of vases painted with Italian lakeside garden scenes,
signed W. Sedgley, dated 1926, shape H313, 34cm high.

Kitty Blake

KITTY BLAKE WORKED at the Royal Worcester factory for 48 years (1905 - 1953). She specialised in flowers and small fruits and several designs of blackberries and buttercups were of her own making. Her Hadley style rendering of bunches of blackberries, evocative of October's misty mornings, have become the Kitty Blake signature pieces and are mouth wateringly realistic.

Like so many other famous ceramic painters, Kitty Blake seems to have come from an artistically talented family. Her brother Edward worked for the Locke factory as a painter of pheasants.

A 'team player' with a keen sense of humour, Kitty Blake was very popular at the Royal Worcester factory and was considered to be a bit of a 'live wire' in her younger days. If the male painters had their 'Terrible Seven' apprentices, the female painters had their 'Saucy Six', who would terrorise any of the male staff. Kitty Blake was a leading light in this group and they made their presence felt both inside and outside the Royal Worcester factory.

Kitty Blake was a driving force at the factory throughout her long stay. Times were hard for much of it and she would spend her spare time making advertising posters for events held at the Royal Worcester works. She is said to have the 'common touch' and is reputed to have never been seen without her red lipstick and a cigarette dangling from her mouth.

A well painted jardinière, signed K. Blake,
dated 1912, shape F132, 15cm high.

Two pot-pourris painted with Autumn fruit, signed K. Blake,
left, dated 1938, shape H169, 17cm high.
right, dated 1925, shape 1314, 14cm high.

Raymond Rushton

BORN IN 1886, Raymond Rushton spent most of his working life as a landscape painter at the Worcester Royal Porcelain Works. He specialised in country mansions, cottages and garden scenes and was a very meticulous artist with great attention to detail. He was well known for his series of Royal Palace gardens in full rich colours and for his castle scenes in black and white.

He often did the colouring in work for plates painted with castles and cathedrals, designed in outline by Harry Davis.

Fond of fishing, he would spend his days off on the river bank, often in the company of William Hawkins. In the evenings, he played the piano for beer money in the public house opposite the factory. To supplement his income in difficult economic times, he became well known for his watercolours, supplying them for Christmas cards and calendar companies.

In his early years, he was a prize winner at the National School of Arts, but he became crippled by arthritis in later years. Even so, he continued painting in excellent style until his retirement in 1953, just three years before his death.

For another example of the work of Raymond Rushton, please see page 159.

Three magnificent plates painted to the centres and outside panels with
Shakespearian views, signed R. Rushton, dated 1920, 27cm wide.
The floral cartouches are signed by E. Phillips.

A very good pair of landscape vases signed R. Rushton,
dated 1919, shape 1481, standing 34cm high.

George Johnson

GEORGE JOHNSON WAS born in 1859 and started at Royal Worcester in 1875.

His main subjects were swans (particularly after the departure of Charles Baldwyn), storks and flamingoes (especially after Walter Powell left) and game birds. George also did exotic birds and reproduction Chamberlain pieces.

A very skilled artist, George also produced many oils and watercolours on canvas and board. He was a great friend of Charles Baldwyn and the two of them would often go on walking and sketching trips into the countryside.

George stayed at the factory throughout his working life and died in 1931.

A fine rose jar painted with storks by George Johnson,
dated 1908, shape 2048, 25cm high.

1265 - what a wonderful shape - painted by George Johnson,
dated 1904, 28cm high.

Frederick Chivers

FREDERICK CHIVERS (1881 - 1965) was one of the many 'wandering' ceramic painters of his time.

He worked as a fruit painter at Royal Worcester from the late 1890s and developed a personal style of painting fruit against a mossy background that had been stippled on with a stick softened by chewing! It may sound unusual but it was certainly very effective.

In 1906, Frederick left Worcester for the Coalport factory in Shropshire where he became one of their highly prized fruit painters. His mossy backgrounds were not so evident here. His paintings were very meticulous and always included any blemishes or bruises that the fruit he was painting contained. It would appear that he preferred to do still life painting from actual arrangements on his desk rather than work from his own mind's eye.

With the exception of a short break for war service, Frederick stayed at Coalport until 1930 when he returned to Worcester for a few years, taking up his fruit painting almost where he had left off.

After only a few years back at Worcester, Frederick was on the move again and this time turned up at the Derby factory where he stayed until his retirement.

He died in 1965 aged eighty four.

A pair of good cobalt blue vases signed F. Chivers,
dated 1905, shape number 1410, standing 29cm high.

John Ayrton

JOHN AYRTON, BROTHER to Harry, was born in 1897. He started at the factory in 1913 and was put under the wing of William Hawkins, emulating many of his still life fruit paintings.

John joined the armed forces in 1915 and served in France. He died shortly afterwards, aged 21, as a result of a horse kicking him in the chest.

Please take the time to study the plate below and realise what a great loss this young man was - he was 16 when he produced this plate and his work rivalled that of his master Hawkins, even at this young age.

His work is extremely rare.

A fantastic still life fruit painting,
signed J. Ayrton, dated 1913, 23cm wide.

Coronation Orbs
– Raymond Rushton and Ernest Barker

A very rare pair of Coronation Orbs brought out to commemorate the
coronation of King George V on June 22 1911, shape 2516, 17cm high.
The orb on the left is signed E. Barker and the right is signed R. Rushton.

George Cole

GEORGE WAS A fine painter of fruit and flowers, with an extensive range of wild flowers which he painted to perfection. He left the factory in the early 1900s and died in 1912. His work is relatively rare.

For other fine examples of Cole's work, please view pages 131 and 147.

A well painted trio signed G. Cole, dated 1907,
shape H166 in the centre and 2441 on each side, 17cm high.

Ernest Phillips

ERNEST PHILLIPS WORKED at the Royal Worcester factory from 1890 and had a brilliant sense of colour and accuracy of touch.

A fine painter, usually doing plate centres or panels on vases with arrangements of flowers, he was a keen horticulturist and often painted studies directly from his own garden. His painting of festoons of flowers can occasionally be seen on some of the reticulated George Owen pieces, although this was more commonly done by Harry Chair.

Ernest Phillips passed away in 1932.

Please view page 24 for another fine example of the work of Ernest Phillips. The fact that he was chosen to decorate such an important vase must surely reflect the esteem the Royal Worcester management held in Ernest Phillips.

A very fine garniture set painted with swags of flowers signed E. Phillips,
dated 1908, shape 2366 in the centre and 2364 on each side, height 20cm.

Henry (Harry) Chair

HARRY CHAIR WAS born in 1858 and worked at the factory for over 42 years from 1872 to 1914.

His main subject was roses and he was regarded by many as the best rose painter of all time.

A lot of Harry's work can be found on George Owen pieces, coming in the form of festoons or swags of flowers to the body of a vase.

He passed away in 1920.

Please view pages 87, 147 and the back cover for other fine examples of the work of Harry Chair.

An excellent pair of cobalt blue vases signed H. Chair,
dated 1903, shape number 1515, standing 21cm high.

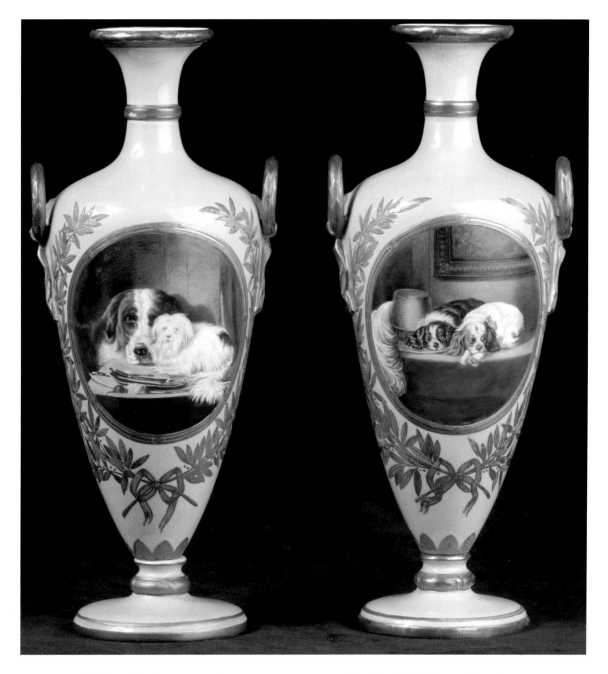

This pair of spectacular vases are very early, dated 1865, attributed to
Josiah Rushton, with scenes after Sir Edwin Landseer, standing 33cm high.

The vase on the left depicts a painting entitled 'The Lion Dog, From Malta' (1830)
– the original is owned by H. R. H. The Duchess of Kent.

The other vase shows a work called 'The Cavalier's Pets' (1845) – the original is in the
Tate Gallery, London. The Cavalier King Charles Spaniel on the left in this painting is
Queen Victoria's favourite pet, 'Dash'.

The gilding is the work of Josiah Davis - the grandfather of Harry Davis.

Ernest Barker

BORN IN 1890, Ernest was working at the Royal Worcester factory by the time he was 12 years old. He trained under Harry Davis and became known for his Highland sheep, English birds and flowers, most of which would appear on smaller pieces and plate centres.

Like the majority of painters working at Worcester during these hard economic times, Ernest would turn to freelance work to raise extra money. There is a large number of excellent water colours bearing his much sought after signature.

He worked at the factory until shortly before his death in 1956.

Please see page 159 for another example of the work of Ernest Barker.

A finely painted tea set depicting English birds,
signed E. Barker, dated 1929.

George Evans

BORN IN 1899, George Evans was an example of several painters who worked at Royal Worcester, left at some stage, and then returned.

A fine landscape painter, George probably started at Worcester before 1920, painting landscapes, particularly in the style of the famous French artist, Corot. He also specialised in the painting of dogs.

He also did filling in work on Walter Sedgley's etchings which he signed 'H. George'.

He left Worcester in the 1930s to go to Royal Doulton but later returned and painted the first runs of the Doughty birds. He died in 1958.

A rare set of coffee cans and saucers painted with spaniels,
signed G. Evans, dated 1934.

James Bradley

JAMES BRADLEY (SENIOR) worked in the 1850s and 1860s, painting Landseer subjects, birds and also pieces in the Birkett Foster style. His son, James Bradley (junior) painted at the factory around the mid to late 1800s. His subjects were dogs, and birds done in a Japanese style.

An unusual pair of plaques painted with birds and ducks by James Bradley, dated 1865, 38cm diameter. These plaques represent a rare collaborative project between father and son as one is painted by James Bradley (senior) and one by James Bradley (junior).

Robert Perling

ROBERT PERLING SPENT around 30 years at the factory from about 1855 to 1885. His speciality was in reproducing on porcelain the work of contemporary artists, Sir Edwin Landseer and T. Sidney Cooper.

A very large and captivating pair of plaques by Robert Perling painted after
Sir Edwin Landseer with scenes depicting deer, dated 1860, 42cm diameter.
The plaque on the right reproduces the famous 'Monarch Of The Glen' (1851) painting
- the original is in the Tate Gallery in London.
The plaque on the left is entitled 'Deer and Deerhounds in a Mountain Torrent' (1833).

William Jarman

WILLIAM STARTED WITH the Worcester firm of Hadleys as a painter of roses but quickly went on to specialise in peacocks, often in a twilight scene.

Following the death of James Hadley and the takeover of his works by Royal Worcester, William moved over to the main factory in the city and stayed there until the start of the First World War when he joined the army.

William returned safely from the war but did not return to porcelain painting, becoming a masseur by profession.

A fine pair of rose painted vases signed W. Jarman,
dated 1912, shape 1969, standing 40cm high.

Harry Martin

VERY LITTLE IS known about Harry Martin. He joined Royal Worcester as a painter of Hadley style roses and peacocks some time before 1914. As he only stayed at the factory for a short time, his work is very scarce. After joining the armed forces in World War One, he was killed in action in Belgium in 1917.

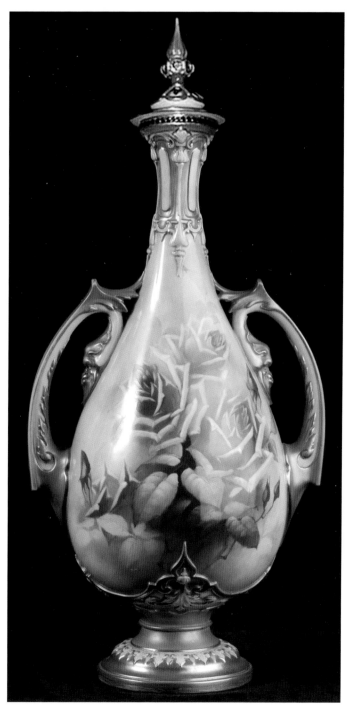

A superb example of roses signed H. Martin,
dated 1908, shape H229, standing 48cm high.

An excellent rose vase painted and signed J. Southall,
dated 1913, shape H248, standing 40cm high.

Charles White

NOT A GREAT deal is known about Charles White. He was born in 1885 and worked for Hadley's in 1900 painting peacock and rose subjects. He then came over to Royal Worcester in the change over and left around 1910 to go to the Royal Doulton factory where he worked for 5 years. He died in 1976.

A fine jardinière painted with roses signed C. White,
dated 1904, shape H168, 23cm high.

VALERIE MAIN

Valerie Main has been established for many years as one of the leading dealers in English porcelain, specialising in Royal Worcester particularly from named artists.

The extensive knowledge built up over the years by the husband and wife team of David and Valerie, ensures that even the most discerning collectors can be assured of quality and service.

Sourcing from all over the world, David and Valerie pride themselves on their range of stock, focusing only on items of the finest quality, and consistently being aware of customers requirements.

Tel 01228 711342
Email valerie.main@btinternet.com

Website www.valeriemain.co.uk

Abcir. Org

Antique British Ceramics Information Resource.

This internet site is a must for all porcelain lovers, developed and updated

by the writer Graham it contains a wealth of information on most of the

British ceramics factories over the last 200 years. The site includes forums

and ceramtique.com which covers items for sale. You will also get an up

to dated E-zine on a regular basis to keep you up to speed.

www.abcir.org

Date Codes for The Golden Years

1892 = 1 dot on left of crown	1917 = * plus 1 dot
1893 = 1 dot each side of crown	1918 = * plus 2 dots
1894 = 3 dots	1919 = * plus 3 dots
1895 = 4 dots	1920 = * plus 4 dots
1896 = 5 dots	1921 = * plus 5 dots
1897 = 6 dots	1922 = * plus 6 dots
1898 = 7 dots	1923 = * plus 7 dots
1899 = 8 dots	1924 = * plus 8 dots
1900 = 9 dots	1925 = * plus 9 dots
1901 = 10 dots	1926 = * plus 10 dots
1902 = 11 dots	1927 = * plus 11 dots
1903 = 12 dots	1928 = An open square □
1904 = 13 dots	1929 = An open diamond ◊
1905 = 14 dots	1930 = a division sign ÷
1906 = 15 dots	1931 = Two touching circles ⊂⊃
1907 = 16 dots	1932 = Three touching circles ⊂⊃⊃
1908 = 17 dots	1933 = Three touching circles and 1 dot
1909 = 18 dots	1934 = Three touching circles and 2 dots
1910 = 19 dots	1935 = Three touching circles and 3 dots
1911 = 20 dots	1936 = Three touching circles and 4 dots
1912 = 21 dots	1937 = Three touching circles and 5 dots
1913 = 22 dots	1938 = Three touching circles and 6 dots
1914 = 23 dots	1939 = Three touching circles and 7 dots
1915 = 24 dots	1940 = Three touching circles and 8 dots
1916 = single * under the circle	1941 = Three touching circles and 9 dots

Index of Shapes

Shape	Page Number	Shape	Page Number	Shape	Page Number
36	93	1970	43	2441	160
763	92	2007	35, 54, 130, 131	2443	139
789	Back cover	2010	33, 44	2448	108
1144	87	2032	138	2450	31
1176	145	2048	13, 68, 76, 111	2510	67
1265	155		115, 127, 154	2516	159
1309	63	2049	123	2713	74
1314	151	2055	48	H157	65
1407	52, 53	2090	24, 25	H166	160
1410	118, 157	2151	62, 120	H168	171
1428	9, 51, 64, Front cover	2158	30	H169	125, 151
1481	153	2217	146, 147	H175	23
1482	97	2256	21	H191	114
1515	19, 36, 37, 40, 136, 162	2305	113	H229	169
1523	69	2307	47	H248	26, 27, 59, 170
1539	41, 90	2330	55	H254	73
1552	89	2336	57, 110	H256	56, 121
1572	22, 46, 75, 109	2337	49	H295	148
1618	38	2354	100	H307	124
1762	23	2363	91	H313	149
1835	45	2364	161	H314	15
1847	129	2366	161	F100	117
1858	126	2401	107	F132	150
1868	133	2406	10, 11	G42	116, 137
1927	42	2416	93	G957	28
1937	104	2425	58	G962	29
1969	12, 14, 17, 60, 61	2430	119		
	99, 103, 132, 168	2432	101		

Index of Artists

Ayrton, John	158	Phillips, Ernest	161
Baldwyn, Charles	32	Powell, Walter	114
Barker, Ernest	164	Powell, William	140
Blake, Kitty	150	Price, Horace	80
Bradley, James	166	Ricketts, William	75
Chair, Harry	162	Roberts, Frank	128
Chivers, Frederick	156	Rushton, Josiah	163
Cole, George	160	Rushton, Raymond	152
Davis, Harry	8	Salter, Edward	144
Evans, George	165	Sebright, Richard	106
Freeman, John	76	Sedgley, Walter	148
Hawkins, William	96	Southall, Jack	170
Jarman, William	168	Stinton, Harry	122
Johnson, George	154	Stinton, James	134
Lockyer, Thomas	78	Stinton, John	50
Martin, Harry	169	Townsend, Edward	73
Owen, George	84	White, Charles	171
Perling, Robert	167		